POETRY FROM CRESCENT
MOON

Edmund Spenser: *Heavenly Love:
Selected Poems*
selected and introduced by Teresa
Page

Edmund Spenser: *Amoretti*
edited by Teresa Page

*The Visions of Petrarch and Bellay:
Early Sonnets*
by Edmund Spenser

Robert Herrick: *Delight In
Disorder: Selected Poems*
edited and introduced by M.K.
Pace

Robert Herrick: *Hesperides*
edited and introduced by M.K.
Pace

Robert Herrick: *Upon Julia's
Breasts: Love Poems*
edited and introduced by M.K.
Pace

Sir Thomas Wyatt: *Love For Love:
Selected Poems*
selected and introduced by Louise
Cooper

John Donne: *Air and Angels:
Selected Poems*
selected and introduced by A.H.
Ninham

D.H. Lawrence: *Being Alive:
Selected Poems*
edited with an introduction by
Margaret Elvy

D.H. Lawrence: *Amores*
edited with an introduction by
Margaret Elvy

D.H. Lawrence: *Look! We Have
Come Through!*
edited with an introduction by
Margaret Elvy

D.H. Lawrence: *Love Poems and
Others*
edited with an introduction by
Margaret Elvy

D.H. Lawrence: *New Poems*
edited with an introduction by
Margaret Elvy

*D.H. Lawrence: Symbolic
Landscapes*
by Jane Foster

*D.H. Lawrence: Infinite Sensual
Violence*
by M.K. Pace

Percy Bysshe Shelley: *Paradise of
Golden Lights: Selected Poems*
selected and introduced by
Charlotte Greene

Thomas Hardy: *Her Haunting
Ground: Selected Poems*
edited, with an introduction by
A.H. Ninham

Thomas Hardy: *Late Lyrics and
Earlier*
edited, with an introduction by
A.H. Ninham

Thomas Hardy: *Moments of
Vision*
edited, with an introduction by
A.H. Ninham

Thomas Hardy: *Poems of the Past
and the Present*
edited, with an introduction by
A.H. Ninham

PAUL VERLAINE

STEFAN ZWEIG

PAUL VERLAINE

BY STEFAN ZWEIG

TRANSLATED BY O.F. THEIS

POEMS TRANSLATED BY ARTHUR SYMONS

EDITED BY ANDREW JARY

CRESCENT MOON

CRESCENT MOON PUBLISHING
P.O. Box 1312, Maidstone
Kent, ME14 5XU
Great Britain
www.crmoon.com

First published 1913. This edition 2025.
Designed by Radiance Graphics.

The right of Andrew Jary to be identified as the editor of *Languorous Ecstasy: Selected Poems* has been asserted generally in accordance with sections 77 and 78 of the Copyright, Designs and Patents Act 1988.

British Library Cataloguing in Publication data

ISBN-13 9781861718082
ISBN-13 9781861710840
ISBN-13 9781861719560

Contents

NOTE ON THE TEXT

The text is from *Paul Verlaine* by Stefan Zweig, translated by O.F. Theis, published by Maunsell and Co., 1913.

The poems are from *The Symbolist Movement In Literature* by Arthur Symons, translated by Arthur Symons, published by E.P. Dutton, New York, 1919.

The French text of the poems is from *Oeuvres Complètes de Paul Verlaine,* published by Vanier, Paris, 1902.

Footnotes are in square brackets: [1]

Paul Verlaine by Eugène Carrière

Jean Frédéric Bazille, Paul Verlaine, 1868

PAUL VERLAINE

PRELUDE

The works of great artists are silent books of eternal truths. And thus it is indelibly written in the face of Balzac, as Rodin has graven it, that the beauty of the creative gesture is wild, unwilling and painful. He has shown that great creative gifts do not mean fulness and giving out of abundance. On the contrary the expression is that of one who seeks help and strives to emancipate himself. A child when afraid thrusts out his arms, and those that are falling hold out the hand to passers-by for aid; similarly, creative artists project their sorrows and joys and all their sudden pain which is greater than their own strength. They hold them out like a net with which to ensnare, like a rope by which to escape. Like beggars on the street weighed down with misery and want, they give their words to passers-by. Each syllable gives relief because they thus project their own life into that of strangers. Their fortune and misfortune, their rejoicing and complaint, too heavy for them, are sown in the destiny of others – man and woman. The fertilizing germ is planted at this moment which is simultaneously painful and happy, and they rejoice. But the origin of this impulse, as of all others, lies in need, sweet, tormenting need, over-ripe painful force.

No poet of recent years has possessed this need of expressing his life to others, more imperatively, pitifully, or tragically than Paul Verlaine, because no other poet was so weak to the press of destiny. All his creative virtue is reversed strength; it is weakness. Since he could not subdue, the plaint alone remained to him; since he could not mould circumstances, they glimmer i naked, untamed, humanly-divine beauty through his work. Thus he has achieved a primæval lyricism – pure humanity, simple complaint, humbleness, infantile lisping, wrath and reproach; primitive sounds in sublime form, like the sobbing wail of a beaten child, the uneasy cry of those who are lost, the plaintive call of the solitary bird which is thrown out into the dusk of evening.

Other poets have had a wider range. There have been the criers who with a clarion horn call together the wanderers on all the highways, the magicians who weave notes like the rustling of leaves, the soughing of winds and the bubbling of water, and the masters who embrace all the wisdom of life in dark sayings. He possessed nothing but the sign-manual of the weak who have need of another, the gestures of a beggar. But in all their accents and nuances, in him, these became wonderful. In him were the low grumbling of the weak man, sometimes closely akin to the sorrowful mumbling of the drunkard, the tender flute notes of vague and melancholic yearning, as well as the hard accusing hammering against his own heart. There were in him the flagellant strokes of the penitent as well as the intimate prayers of thanksgiving which poor women murmur on church steps. Other poets have been so interwoven with the universal that it is impossible to distinguish whether really great storms trembled in their breasts, whether the sea rolled within them, or again, whether it was not their words, which made the meadows shudder, and which, as a breeze, went tenderly over the fields. They were the vivifying poets, the synthesizers – divinities by the marvel of creation, and its priests.

Verlaine was always only a human being, a weak human being, who did not even know how "to count the transgressions of his own heart." It was this very lack of individuality, however, which produced something much rarer – the purely and entirely human. Verlaine was soft clay without the power of producing impresses and without resistance. Thus every line of life crossing his destiny has left a pure relief, a clear and faithful reproduction, even to the fragrance-like sorrows of lonely seconds which in others fade away or thicken into dull grief. The tangled forces which tempestuously shook his life and tore it to tatters crystallized in his work and were distilled into essences.

This, together with the fact that he has enriched and furthered literary development by his poetry, is the highest and noblest meed of praise that can be given to a poet. Yet such an estimate seems too low to many of his followers, especially the more recent French literati who celebrate in Verlaine the unconscious inventor of a new art of poetry and the initiator of new lyric epochs, unknowing of the folly of their proceeding.

Verlaine, the literary man, was a sad caricature distorted by ribald noise and Quartier-Latin cafés. Even as such he indignantly denied this intention. The greatness and power of his lyricism takes its root in eternity, in the wonderful sincerity of its ever human and unalterable emotional content, and above all in the unconsciousness of its genesis.

Intellectuals alone create "tendencies." Verlaine was as little one of these as he was on the other hand the *bon enfant*, the innocently stumbling child into whose open and playful hand verses fell like cherry blossoms or fluttering leaves. He was a lyric poet. Lyricism is thinking without logic (although not contrary to logic), association not according to the laws of thought but according to intuition, the whispering words of vague emotions, hidden correspondences, darkly murmuring subterranean streams. Lyricism again is thought without consequence, instinct and presentiment, leaping quickly in lawless synthesis; it is union but not a chain formed of individual links, it is melody but not scales. In this sense he was an unconscious creator who heard great accords.

He was never a thinker. His quick power of observation, flashing electrically, his Gallic wit, and his exquisite feeling for style were able to illumine splendidly, narrow circles, but he lacked, as in everything, the power and ability of logical sequence. He knew how to seize and throw light upon waves that came to touch his life, but he could not make them reflect in the dark mirror of the universe, nor could he throw out into the world rays of curious and tormenting desire for life. He could not construct a world vision, revolution, and a sense of distance. This wild and heroic trait of the great poets was never his. He preferred, fleeting and weak spirit as he was, the indefinite, not quiet and possession, nor understanding and power, which are the elemental factors of life. He surrendered himself completely to the efflorescence of things, to the sweetness of becoming and the sadness of evanescence, to the pain and tenderness of emotions that touch us in passing; in short, to the things that come to us and not to those which we must seek and strive to penetrate. He was never a drawn bow ready to fling himself as an arrow into the infinite; he was only an æolian harp, the play and voice of such winds as came. Unresistingly he threw himself into the arms of all dangers – women, religiosity, drunkenness and literature. All this oppressed him and rent him asunder. The drops of blood are magnificent poems, imperishable events, primæval human emotion clear as crystal.

Two factors were responsible for this: an unexampled candor in both virtue and vice, and his complete unconsciousness, which, however, was unfortunately lost in the first waves of his fame. As he never knew how to weed, his life forced strange blossoms and became a wonderful garden of seductively beautiful, perversely colored flowers, among which he himself was never entirely at home. In middle life he found the courage, or rather an impulse within him mightier than his will forced him to do so, and with relentless tread he left civilization. He exchanged the warm cover of an established literary reputation for the occasional shelter along the highways. With the smoke of his pipe he blew into the air the esteem he had acquired early. He never returned to the safe harbor. Later, as "man of letters," he unfortunately exaggerated this as well as every other of his unique characteristics, in an idle exhibitionism, and made literary use of them.

Far distant from academies and journals, he retained his uniqueness uninterruptedly for many years. He has described in his verses the errant and passionate way of his life with that noble absence of shame which is the first sign of personal emancipation from civilized humanity, in contrast to the primitively natural.

Much has been said and written as to whether happiness or unhappiness was the result of the pilgrimage. It is an unimportant and idle question, because "happiness" is only a word, an unfilled cup in strange hands, and an empty tinkling thing. At any rate, life cut more deeply into his flesh than into that of any other poet of our time. So tightly and pitilessly was his soul wound about that nothing was kept silent, and it bled to death with sighs, rejoicings, and cries. A destiny which has accomplished such marvels may be rebuked as cruel. But we in whom these pains re-echo in sweet shudderings – for us, it is fitting that we should feel gratitude.

CONCERNING "POOR LELIAN"[1]

Whenever Verlaine speaks of his childhood, there is a gleam like a bittersweet smile. This hesitant, plaintive rhythm appears ever, and ever again, whether in sorrow, musing sigh, or plaintive reproach. It appears in the tender and so infinitely sad lines which he wrote in prison, and likewise in the *Confessions*, a vain, exaggeratedly candid and coquetting portrait in prose. Gentle memories, fresh and tender like white roses, creep loosely through all his work, scattering pious fragrance. For him childhood was paradise, because his poor weak soul, needing the tenderness of faithful hands, had not yet experienced the hard impacts of life, but only the soft intimate cradling between devoted love and womanly mildness – a lulling, sweet unforgettable melody.

All impulses are still pure and bud-like. Love is unsullied, sheer instinct, entirely without desire and restlessness. It is silence, peaceful silence, cool longing which assuages, and so all of life is kind and large, maternal and womanly – soft. Everything shines in a clear, transparent, shimmering light like a landscape at daybreak. Even late, very late, when his poor life had already become barren and over-clouded, this yearning still rises and trembles toward these days of youth like a white dove. The "*guote suendaere*" still had tears to give. Gleaming pure like dew drops, and still fresh, they cling to the most fantastic and wildest blooms.

The first dates tell little. Paul Marie Verlaine was born in 1844 at Metz – he did not remember his second name until the appropriate time of his conversion. His father was a captain in the French engineer corps. Verlaine, however, was not of Alsatian extraction but belonged to Lorraine, close enough to Germany to bear in his blood the secret fructification of the German *Lied*. Early in his life the family removed to Paris, where the attractive boy with inquisitive, soft face (as is shown on an early photograph) soon turns into a *gosse* and finally into a government official with skillful literary talents.

Several pleasing episodes and a few kind figures are found within this simple frame of his external life. Two in particular are drawn in subdued delicate colors and veiled with a tender fragrance. Both were women. His mother, all goodness and devotion, spoiling him with too much tenderness and forgiveness, passes through his life with uniformly quiet tread; she is a wonderfully noble martyr. There is hardly a more poignant story than the one he tells regretfully in the *Confessions* of the time when he first began to drink and how his mother never voiced her reproach. Once when with hat on his head he had slept out the remainder of a wild night, her only comment was the silent one of holding a mirror before him.

And there is no more tragic incident among the many sentences of the drunkard than the verdict of the tribunal at Vouziers, which condemned him to a fine of five hundred francs for threatening to kill his mother. Even then, though absinthe had changed the simple child always ready for penance into a different man, her gesture was still the noble and inimitable one of forgiveness.

There were also other tender hands to watch over his youth. His cousin Eliza, who died early, is a figure so mild and transparent and of so light a tread that she appears like one of Jacobsen's wonderful creations who wander and speak like disembodied souls. She had the unique beauty of early illness, and on that account perhaps turned more toward the absorbed but not melancholy child, excusing his escapades. She was loved tenderly, with a child's love that was without desire and danger.

> "Certes oui pauvre maman était
> Bien, trop bonne, et mon cœur à la voir palpitait,
> Tressautait, et riait et pleurait de l'entendre
> Mais toi, je t'aimais autrement non pas plus tendre
> Plus familier, voilà."

It was she too who staged his last youthful folly by giving him the money for printing the *Poèmes Saturniens*. Like a white flame her figure shines through the dense stifling fumes of his life. It is as if the soft tread of these two women had given many of his verses their seraphic sheen and lent the mother-of-pearl opalescence to his softest poems, in which there is a secret rustling as of the folds of women's gowns. Even the Paul Verlaine of the later years, "the ruin insufficiently ruined," who saw in woman the most ferocious enemy, and who fled to the wolves that they might protect him from "woman their sister," even he still dreamed of the folded hands, of the forgiving innocent gesture of the earliest memories. This yearning for mild and pure women has found many incarnations. In the poems to his bride, Mathilde Manté, it is the tender song of the troubadour; in the hours of his mystical conversion it becomes a tender prayer and Madonna cult; in the years of his decadence it appears as a pathetic echo, a stumbling plaint and dreamy childhood desires – the precious hour between sin and sin. Sometimes this secret desire is placed tenderly and simply into lines of verse as into a rare, fragrant shrine where the dearest possessions are kept. These are pure, wonderful lines like the following, full of longing and renunciation:

> "Je voudrais, si ma vie était encore à faire,
> Qu'une femme très calme habitât avec moi."

Verlaine soon left these mirror-clear days of beautiful youth. His father decided to put him into a boarding-school at Paris. The dreamy little boy, looking toward the gay school cap, gladly assented. This was the turning point. Here his life in a way was rent in two parts, and a wide gap appears in the weakly but not morbid character of the child. The somewhat spoiled, modest, and confiding boy is put among students who are already dissolute and overbearing. On the very first day he is sickened by the coldness and barrenness of the rooms, and frightened by the first contact with life he is instinctively afraid of the evil which was to overtake him after all. Filled with that mighty longing for tenderness and gentle shelter which even at fifty he did not lose, he fled to his home in tears. He was greeted there with cries of joy and embraces, but on the next morning he was taken back with gentle force.

This was the catastrophe. Verlaine's weak character willingly submitted to foreign influences; it became dulled under the influence of his comrades, "and the overthrow began." A foreign element entered his being, a materialistic cynical trait, for the present only *gaminerie*, while he was still a stranger to sex. The specific Parisian character, a mingling of vanity, insolence, scoffing wit (*raillerie*) and boastful bravado, tempted the soft dreamy boy, but conquered him only for short hours.

This conflict between feminine sensitivity and a *gaminerie* eager for enjoyment wages incessant warfare throughout his life. Sometimes it harmonizes for brief moments voluptuousness and idealism, but neither side ever wins and the struggle never ceases. The characteristics of Faust and Mephistopheles never became fully linked in Verlaine; they only interlaced. With the overpowering capacity for self-surrender which he spent on everything, he could combine the sensual alone or the spiritual alone completely with his life, but lacking will, he was unable to put an end to the constant rotation, which now dragged him in penitence from his passions only to hurl him back again into their hated hands. Thus his life consists not of an evenly ascending plane, but of headlong descents and catastrophes, of elevations and transfigurations, which finally end in a great weariness.

The sense of shame was exceptionally strong in him, as it is in every case where it is repressed. All his life long it made itself heard in the form of yearning for clarity and purity. Afraid of mockery, cynicism and indifference were put forward as a protection until at length these evil influences overgrew it entirely. Were it not unwise to reflect in directions which his life disdained to follow, it might be interesting to attempt a portrait of Verlaine as he might have been if he had continued on the luminous path of his childhood under the guidance of kind hands. For surely and also according to his own opinion, those years were the humus for the *fleurs du mal* of his soul.

In these formative years of ungainly figure and uncertain dreaming the poet grows out of the boy. A malign influence, puberty, forces the creator in him. "The man of letters, let us say rather, if you prefer, the poet was born in me precisely toward that so critical fourteenth year, so that I can say proportionately as my puberty developed my character too was formed." This is surely a womanly and feminine trait, for in women the entire spiritual development usually trembles as the resonance of the inner shock. Physical crises are transformed into catastrophes of the soul, and the pressure of the blood and its beating waves are spiritualized into the soft melancholy and sweet dreams from which his verses rise like tender buds.

It is not out of intellectual growth or out of the persistent impulse to link the universal to his personality, as in the cases of Schiller, Victor Hugo or Lord Byron, that these soft notes rise. They have their origin in a sultry restlessness of the nerves, in the well-springs of fruitful impulse, in emotions and shadowy presentiments. They are the early outpouring of creative masculinity and youthful yearning. They are half a question and half an answer to life. They are melancholy and vague, filled with uncertain gleaming and a rustling darkness. If poetry consists in a certain sensitiveness of soul and reaction to slight and cautious

✳ 27

stimulation, and not in an active, wild, subduing force, Verlaine certainly has sensed the deepest fount of the orphic mysteries. If poetry is so understood, the boy who wrote the *Poèmes Saturniens* on his school benches, already saw the reality of life and even the future mask. His acute ear heard the oracle which foretold his destiny, but he did not know how to interpret what the Pythian voice had whispered until everything was fulfilled. To understand this, sensitiveness must not be confused with sentimentality. Sentimentality may grow out of a pessimism which has been acquired intellectually. Sensitivity is not only the child of emotion but at the same time the sum and substance of all feelings. It is both an inherent tendency and an innate possession, and is primæval and indestructible as is the gift of poetry itself. The gift of poetry implies the power of distilling emotions into that form in which they are already essentially existing and fixing the fleeting and ephemeral permanently as by a chemical process which knows no law but only presentiment and chance.

There is, of course, no art without its technique, understanding technique not in the derogatory sense of a mere implement but somewhat in the sense of the material which the painter uses, who must apply it individually and thus adds something unknown and unique to what he has acquired by education and copying. Verlaine learned his technique early, and he never wrote a line in which his own guidance could be felt. His earliest teachers were Baudelaire, Banville, Victor Hugo, Catulle Mendès and other Parnassiens, cool idealists or frosty exotics, measured and stiff even in their melancholy, but wise architects of slender and firmly founded verse-structures, artists in language, chisellers of form. The pliant, soft yielding manner of Verlaine quickly embraced their influences. The student is already master of the *métier*. Even the relentless and unhappy rhymester into which "poor Lelian" turned, late, very late in his career, retained this eminent skill of reproducing forms smoothly and precisely, and writing verses of an agreeable, melodic flow and a beautiful rhythmic movement.

The years of puberty were the time of the production of the *Poèmes Saturniens*. Sexuality had not yet developed sufficiently and was not strong and self-willed enough to operate destructively. Its influence was only felt in slight impacts and produced the feeling of sweet unrest. This unrest, somewhat veiled and turning toward melancholy, trembles through these early poems and lends them the unique beauty of sad women. All the art of Verlaine's poetry is already found in these first poems.

The book appeared, thanks to the assistance of his cousin Eliza, under Lemerre's imprint, curiously enough on the same day as François Coppée's first work, and had a *"joli succès de hostilité"* with the press. The great writers – Victor Hugo, Leconte de Lisle, Theodore de Banville, and others – wrote him encouraging letters, but the public at large did not overburden the young man with its admiration.

At that time Verlaine was a clerk in the Hôtel de Ville and lived a quiet, almost well-to-do life, with his mother. All the indications were in favor of a smooth, unclouded future. But there was a conflict in him, which he could not master. It is like raising and lowering two weights which he never succeeds in balancing. On the one hand is the passionate, wild, sexual element, the impure glow and the blind surrender, the "black ship which drags him to the abyss," and, on the other, the pure, simple, tender mode of his child-like heart, which, a stranger to all passion, yearns for soft, womanly hands.

In normal sexuality the yearning of the senses and the soul unite during the seconds of intoxication and become the symbol of infinity, through the passionate absorption of contrasts and the permeation of spirit with matter, and form with substance, elements which in their turn are the creative symbols of all life. In Verlaine, however, there was always a cleft: now he is pure pilgrim of yearning, now roué; now priest, now gamin. He has wrought the most beautiful religious poems of Catholicism, and at the same time has won the crown of all pornographic works with perverse and indecent poems. As the flux of his blood went, so was he – a *pure reflex of his organic functions*. That is to say he was infinitely primitive as a poet, and infinitely complicated and unaccountable as a human being.

Whenever his impulses were elastic and his senses sharpened or stimulated, the untamed and wild beast of sensuality is unchained in his life, turbulent after satisfaction, incapable of restraint by intellectual deliberation. After the crisis physical exhaustion disengaged the psychic elements of penitence, consideration and tender longing, which later became piety.

Verlaine was a poet of rare candor and shamelessness, both in the best and worst sense. This is the essentially great element in his otherwise feminine, weak and absolutely *negative* personality. The primæval powers of the body and soul are the eternal elements of all humanity and the starting-point of all philo-sophies; the conflict between them, betrayed in the accusing and self-revealing manner of his verse, is transferred unchanged into his poetry, filling it with the force of life and the tragedy of the universally human.

In his entire life there seem to have been only two brief periods of cessation in the struggle; during the short honeymoon or period of normal sexuality and during his first religious epoch, when he was sincere, and enthusiasm and yearning, transfused in the symbols of faith and religious veneration, interpenetrated and inflamed each other.

The *Fêtes Galantes* were published soon after the *Poèmes Saturniens*. Artistically they are far superior, because their form is more individual, their structure more original, and their architecture more compact. Yet they do not appear to me to represent balance, but rather the short trembling, to-and-fro wavering of the scales of his impetuous and sensitive character.

They are coquettish; and coquetry is sensuality with style, tamed accordingly, but not conquered. They are at the same time modest and impudent, attack and careful retreat. They are not pure sensuality, but desire, masked by a demand for modesty.

It is the most characteristically French of his books, drawn as with the maliciously kind brush of Watteau. In these poems, in which Verlaine's muse trips on high-heeled shoes through gardens which shimmer in the gleam of a mocking moon, in these whispering dialogues between Pierrots and Columbines, in these gallant landscapes, an anxious presentiment weeps plaintively in the bushes. This sad mode makes the dallying faces gleam underneath tears. The true voice of the yearning soul is poured out and dies away in the imperishable *Colloque Sentimental*, a dark pearl of indefinite, infinite sorrow. Out of masks and pantomimes, the poet's face stares sadly bewildered into the black mirror of reality.

At that time an evil influence had broken into his life, perhaps the most destructive, "the one unpardonable vice," as he himself confesses. Verlaine began to drink. At first it was bravado, recklessness, persuasion; later it was desire, torture, flight from the qualms of his conscience, "the forgetfulness, sought in execrable potions."

He drank absinthe, a sweetish, greenish liquid, which is false as cat's eyes and treacherous and murderous like a diseased harlot. Baudelaire's hashish is comprehensible. It was the magician who raised fantastic landscapes, it quieted the nerves, it was the poet of the poet. Verlaine's absinthe is only destructive and obliterating, a slow poison which does not kill but unnerves and undermines like the white powders the dreaded secret of which the Borgias held. Absinthe wrought silently and inexorably in Verlaine's life. By degrees it absorbed the tender, soft, yearning, vague qualities of his heart of a child; it made the hard, passionate, depraved man strong, and awakened the sensualist and cynic in him. Even when the high-arched churches and the figures of the Madonnas no longer offered him a place of refuge, "the atrocious green sorceress" was still his only comforter, into whose arms he willingly cast himself.

He himself tells regretfully how at the time of his cousin

Eliza's death, soon after the appearance of his first book, he joined sorrow and vice in tragic manner. For two days he had not touched food. But he drank, drank without interruption, restlessly, and returned to the offices a drunkard, drowning the reproof of his superior in a new absinthe. Everything that was hard, bitter, wild, which later broke loose in him so tempest-uously, compelling the law to step between him and his wife, his mother and his friends, was called forth by the green poison in the silent, kindly nature which loved soft words and was inclined even to his last years to the power of hot tears. With pitiless force this most dangerous of his vices drew taut the chain, by which the passions and sudden catastrophe of his destiny dragged him on to the road of misery.

For a moment it seemed as if everything were to come to a good end. He fell in love with the explosive vehemence and despairing persistence with which the weak are accustomed to cling to an idea. The step-sister of his friend, de Sivry, had fascinated him. As a matter of fact the engagement came about. In these days, separated from his bride, Verlaine wrote the slender volume of songs, *La Bonne Chanson*. It is his most quiet and balanced book. According to his own repeatedly expressed opinion, he considered it the most beautiful of his works and the one dearest to him. In the best and noblest sense they are "occasional verses." Almost daily one is written and sent to his beloved. It was only in small selection that they were united in print.

Here the idea of modesty subdues passion like a wonderful sordine, and surrender and tenderness intertwine with the ideals of modesty. The cleft in Verlaine's personality closes in the consonance of a soul which has found peace. It represents the first period of peace in his life and career and is humanly his most perfect moment and poetically his purest. Vice and passion have disappeared in a hesitating yet desirous surrender, melancholy has dissolved in melody.

Victor Hugo, the sovereign coiner of great phrases, called the *Bonne Chanson*, "*une fleur dans un obus.*" There are poems in this slim volume which seem as if they had been woven out of the gushing flood of moonlight. There are poems which gleam like pale pearls and lonely pools. Word and sense, form and emotion, foreboding and being, life and dreams, are their woof. Here appeared that marvel of French lyric poetry, the wonderful poem.

"La lune blanche
Luit dans les bois;
De chaque branche
Part une voix
Sous la ramée....

"Oh bien-aimée!
"L'étang reflète,
Profond miroir,
La silhouette
Du saule noir
Où le vent pleure ...
"Rêvons: c'est l'heure.
"Un vaste et tendre
Apaisement
Semble descendre
Du firmament
Que l'astre irise ...
"C'est l'heure exquise."

From this point on the life-story in which the germ and seed of such wonderful fruit ripened is painful. The descent was not sudden. Verlaine was one of those wavering characters who require energetic impulsion for good as well as for evil. He never slid as on an inclined plane, but he sank like a scale weighed down by something unsuspected. Thus it is possible to name the catastrophes and to set the milestones of his misfortunes.

The great wrench which in 1870 shook his country, also affected his life and tore it apart. His wedding occurred during the days of the war. The fever of political over-excitement seized him and he, the almost bourgeois government clerk who never troubled about politics, became a communist as a favor to several friends. The anecdote that he once wished to assassinate Emperor Napoleon III was a hoax which he told his comrades for the sake of the sensation, something like the story which Baudelaire told of the "savoriness" of embryonal brains.

His work consisted in reading the articles on the Commune which appeared in the newspapers and marking them whether they were favorable or unfavorable. Nevertheless this insignificant part, which he himself did not take seriously and spoke of as "This stupid enough rôle which I played during two months of illusions," cost him his position. This was the break with well-ordered life and the sign-post which showed him the way into the Bohème.

The old wounds re-opened. Verlaine began to drink again during his activities in the Commune. Recriminations and scenes rose as the result of this relapse. Suddenly came the decisive act of the drunkard; he struck his wife the first blow. New misunderstandings followed, but the household still held together, soon to be increased by the arrival of a son.

The final element is still lacking. Abstractions are weak against realities, things that have happened may change men but they cannot vanquish them. So far everything has been only inchoate power and a foreshadowing threat, but not enchantment. It is only the magic of a passion, an elemental and unfathomable magnetic power which links one human being to another, the intangible, which can conquer a poet. He can overcome want and life because he despises them; he can make evil powerless because he repents; chance he can bridge; but he cannot hold back destiny, nor win battles with the incomprehensible.

A new influence enters Verlaine's life – Arthur Rimbaud.

THE RIMBAUD EPISODE

No matter how much a writer may have striven for the unusual or have tried to order confusing ways with intelligence and form, his fiction does not reach the depths nor is it as tragic as this one which life devised. The beginning is simple, the climax grandiose, of such wildness and rising to such heights, that the end no longer could be pure tragedy. It turned into tragi-comedy, that grotesque sensation which we feel when destiny grows beyond human beings and over-towers them, while they are still struggling with pigmy hands to master a monstrous force which has long gone beyond their control.

The beginning was conventional. One day Verlaine received a letter from an acquaintance in the provinces, in which poems by a fifteen-year-old boy were enclosed. Verlaine's opinion was asked. The poems were: *Les Effarés*, *Les Assis*, *Les Poètes de sept ans*, *Les Premières communions*. Every one knows they were Arthur Rimbaud's, for the poems of this boy are among the most precious of French literature. He began where the best stop and then, at twenty, threw literature aside as something irksome and unimportant. Verlaine read them and was filled with enthusiasm. He wrote to the boy in a tone of glowing admiration. In the meantime the poems made the rounds in Paris. Words of characteristically French emphasis are quickly coined. Victor Hugo with his regal gesture declared the author to be "*Shakespeare enfant.*"

The provincial associations of Charleville filled Rimbaud with disgust and unrest. Verlaine in his enthusiasm wrote to him "Come, dear great soul, we are waiting for you, we want you."

He himself was without a position and his own life in Paris at that time was threatened with chaos and uncertainty, but with the marvellous folly of yielding and emotional natures he invited a stranger as guest into his shaken destiny.

Rimbaud came. He was a big, robust fellow filled with a demonic physical force like that which Balzac has breathed into his Vautrin types. He was a provincial with massive red fists and the curious face of a child that has been corrupted early in life – a gamin, but a genius. Everything in him is force, over-abundant, wild, exceptional virility, without aim and turned toward the infinite.

He is one of the conquistador type, who first lost his way in literature. He pours everything into it, fire, fulness, force, more, much more than great creators spend. Like a crater he throws out his mad fever dreams and visions of life such as perhaps only Dante has had before him. He hurls everything up into the infinite as if he would shatter it to bits. Destruction teems in this creation, a force ardent for power, a hand that would seize everything and crush it.

His poems are only sudden gestures of wrath. They resemble bloody tatters of raw flesh that have been torn with wild teeth from the body of reality. It is poetry "outside and above" all literature. Has there ever been a poet of modern times who thus threw poems on paper and then let the scraps flutter to the four winds? Without pose, unlike Stefan George or Mallarmé, who calculate carefully, he despised the public and literature. He never had a single line printed by his own efforts, he was utterly regardless of the fleeting examples of his gigantic power. At twenty he left his fame and companions behind to wander through the world. In Africa he founded fantastic realms, he sat in prison and there played a part in world history preparing under King Menelik for the struggle which cost Italy her provinces. But in three years he wrote many poems full of power and fire, including the eternal poem *Le bateau ivre*, a staggering fever dream, into which all the colors, sounds, forms and forces of life seem to have been poured, bubbling in curious forms and seething in the glow of a feverish moment. His life was like a dream, as wild, as mighty and as little subject to time.

Verlaine gladly sheltered the awkward boy. Madame Verlaine was less enthusiastic and never concealed her dislike. Perhaps, with a woman's instinct, she unconsciously foresaw the danger which threatened Verlaine in this new companion.

The bond of friendship grew closer and closer. Verlaine's *gaminerie* which was ever in contrast with his sensitivity, awakened suddenly. His tendency toward strong, cynical and lascivious conversation met a genial match in Rimbaud. The primitive element in Verlaine was suddenly enchained by the primæval, purely human and brutal masculinity of Rimbaud's personality. The feminine in his nature was feeling for completion. As if predestined for each other for years, their personalities dovetail. Without any affection, by necessity rather than by friendship, their union becomes closer and closer. One day in 1872 Verlaine leaves wife, child and the world in which he lived to wander with Rimbaud into the unknown.

Without doubt there was an element of the abnormal in the relations between Verlaine and Rimbaud, but to understand their friendship it is neither necessary nor essential to know whether the dangerous potentialities that inhere in so strong a personal enthusiasm ever became material facts.

Their path led over the highways and also through prisons. "An evil rage for travelling" had seized the two. Through Belgium, through Germany and England they wandered; usually they were without means. They stayed in London for a while, supporting themselves by teaching languages and delving deeper than ever into social politics. Rimbaud left and returned just in time to convey the sick Verlaine home. The terrible life which he had led had broken him down. He himself has concealed the tragic incidents of those days in a novelette, "*Louise Leclercq.*"

There he wrote: "The few half-crowns which he earned daily in giving lessons, they spent in the evening on Portuguese wine and Irish beer. The stomach was forgotten, the head became affected and the lessons were not given, and thus hunger and nervosity overcame the reason of this brave fellow."

The patient is taken to Bouillon, a small town in the Ardennes, where Charles van Lerberghe, the great Belgium poet, lived, but he has hardly half recovered when he plunges out into the world again with Rimbaud. Mental unrest is transformed into physical unrest. The lack of stability which operated most impulsively in that crisis, appears in his external life. There is nothing definite for which he is seeking yet he is unsatisfied. Verlaine, man of moods *par excellence*, adjusts himself to life in his own manner. He becomes boorish, subject to fits of passion, violent and unaccountable. His tenderness seems to have been strangled by hunger, drunkenness and wild destiny. The friendship for Rimbaud also assumes evil shapes. More and more frequently they quarrel; almost every hour Rimbaud's foaming temperament and Verlaine's temporary hard, wild manner come in conflict. Of course, as a rule, they were drunk. Rimbaud, who was strong, drank because of his feeling of strength and because he yearned for the intoxication in which colors glowed, in which impulses became wilder, and association more rapid, acute and bolder. Verlaine fled to absinthe to drown out repentance, anguish and weakness; and from this sweetish drink, in which all the evil forces of life seem to be distilled, he drew brutality and feverish disorders.

Once Verlaine ran away, but became repentant and asked Rimbaud to join him. Rimbaud followed him to Belgium. All difficulties were about to be solved. Madame Verlaine was ready to forgive and was on her way to meet the penitent. Then

Rimbaud too declared that he would leave him. No one knows how it happened, whether it was jealousy, anger, hatred, love or only drunkenness, at any rate the disaster followed on the public street of Brussels. Verlaine pursued Rimbaud and shot at him twice with a revolver, wounding him once. The police came, and though Rimbaud defended and excused Verlaine, the latter was arrested. The sentence was two years in prison, and these Verlaine spent at Mons. The immediate result was a divorce, upon which Madame Verlaine insisted with every possible emphasis and in spite of Victor Hugo's intervention.

This conclusion, however, was too banal and trite for so heroic a tragedy. The friendship persisted. Verlaine and Rimbaud corresponded. Verlaine sent occasional poems from prison and told Rimbaud of his conversion. The latter hardly pleased Rimbaud, who was at that time cold and indifferent toward everything except that he was filled with a thirst for something unique and infinite and looking forward to new adventures. Verlaine had hardly been released before he tried to convert Rimbaud to this religious life in order to link their lives anew. "Let us love each other in Jesus Christ," he wrote in his proselyting ardor and with the enthusiasm which in the beginning he always felt for everything. Rimbaud smiled mockingly and finally declared that "Loyola" should visit him in Stuttgart.

Now the moment arrived when comedy outdid the tragedy of the reunion. Verlaine arrived at Stuttgart and attempted the conversion – unfortunately in an inn, a place little adapted for proselytes and prophets, for both the saint and the mocker still had in common their passion for drink. No one witnessed the scene; only the result is known. On the way home both were drunk, and a quarrel ensued and a unique incident in the history of literature followed.

In the flooding moonlight by the banks of the Neckar the two greatest living poets in France fell upon each other in wild rage with sticks and fists. The struggle did not last long. Rimbaud, athletic, like a wild animal, a man of passion, easily subdued the nervous, weakly Verlaine, stumbling in drunkenness. A blow over the head knocked him down. Bleeding and unconscious, he remained lying on the bank.

It was the last time they saw each other. Verlaine disappeared on the next day. The episode had come to an end, but nevertheless several letters passed back and forth. Then Rimbaud's grandiose Odyssey through the entire world began. For many years his friends in Paris believed him dead, and even to-day relatively little is known of his life afterward.[2]

In Vienna he was under arrest as a vagrant, in the Balkans he was a merchant. Then fulfilling his early prophecy in the *Bateau ivre* he said farewell to Europe and in Africa became discoverer, general, conqueror. In these unexpected fields he spent to the last limits his titanic energy, which in youthful crises had been expended on the fragile and for him too weakly material of language and rhyme. Until the day of his death, he, *the only true despiser of literature of these days*, never wrote another line, and endeavored only to give form to his wild and fantastic dreams in the material of life, dying in fever as feverishly he lived.

For Verlaine it was an episode – the most important, it is true, in a life which was torn to many tatters. After his conversion, which will be discussed more fully later, he returned to Paris and literature, and died in harness, physically in 1896, as artist much earlier.

THE PENITENT

It is well known that at the moment when he left the prison at Mons, Paul Verlaine, the prisoner, entered the ranks of the great Catholic poets. A complete transformation took place in his life. He turned from the material to the spiritual. The penitent mood of his childhood days glimmered again when he thought of the Nazarene. The soft early yearnings which were forgotten in his years of wandering became symbolized into a definite idea. Nor is this surprising in one who never could understand his intellectual processes, but who was moved entirely by the ebb and flow of emotion, and who always wavered unsteadily in all the crises of life.

In general it is almost a necessity among poets that poetic feeling should be transmuted into religious feeling.

But the creative poets of active mentality and intellectuality build their own religion, while the sensitive or passive poets pour out their flood of feeling for God in the form of existing rites and symbols. Balzac clearly shows this relationship when he says in *The Thirteen*:

> "Are not religion, love and poetry, the threefold expression of the same fact, the need for expression which fills every noble soul? These three creative impulses rise up toward God, who concentrates in himself all earthly emotions."

✳ 43

Religion is only a certain form of association in which things are placed in relationship with each other. Similarly the sensation of evening, of the cool pure air after rain, of the whispering of the winds and the play of clouds, or whatever else is caught up in the nervous fever of poetic sensibility, hearkens back to the infinite after it has been permeated by the poet's own sorrow or joy. He feels that the infinite has a soul which understands and atones for all sorrows, and thus he conceives it as divinity. The poet's religion is derived from the one great faith with which he must be filled, which is the necessity for being understood. It is only one step further when he finds that his soul's outflow must lead somewhere, and then he gives a name, a form and an interpretation to what has been incomprehensible.

But a more definite element in Paul Verlaine drove him into the arms of Catholicism. It was his *impulse to confession*, which I have tried to show was the most intensive element in his personality. A soul which lacks ethical authority for self-control, in its helplessness must turn with accusation and pleading toward others, toward something outside of the self.

Cry and sigh are the original forms of all lyricism, and just as they are a sweet compulsion to expel an inner overflow by utterance, so confession is only deliverance from an inner pressure, from guilt and penitence, from mighty forces, accordingly, which the confessor wishes to transmit to others. It is a need for explanation, a marvellous deception, a means to tame forces by trust, a trust which is not felt toward one's self. Goethe's much-quoted words of the fragments of the "great confession" are still to the point, no matter how often they have been used. As he wrote to rid his mind of incidents which he had experienced, so Verlaine told of himself, now to the public, now to the confessor. The fundamental process, however, is identical.

Many other things coöperated. There was the great antithesis between flesh and spirit, between body and soul; contempt for the sensual and continual fall into sin – the immanent conflict of childish and animal feeling which flooded forever wildly through

Verlaine's years of manhood. This also has been for centuries the symbol of the Catholic Church. In it sensitive and mystical emotion found a dogmatic form, through the fundamental principle of the antithesis between the earthly and the transcendental. In the same way the consciousness of the value of the sensual as sin and of the pure as virtue is only a reflex of the subjective impressions of pure souls. Here Verlaine found a definite form for the warning which flickered unsteadily in him. By confession he was able to place his sins into the dreamy hands of the immaculate Virgin; in her form he was at last able worthily to give substance to the dream-like shadows of the soft unsensual women, which glimmered like stars over his life. It was the need for quiet after storms, confession after sins.

Childhood bells called him back to the church. Pale ancient memories led him – the pomp of the solemn great processions which he saw in Montpellier. The *bon enfant* awoke in him again. The memory of his own folded hands, of his timid child's voice lisping prayers, and of his sacred soft baptismal name, *Marie*, rose in him. The dark mysticism and the wonderful blue half-lights of Catholic faith called the dreamer. The same incense shadow of vague violent emotion led the romantic dreamers, Stolberg, Schlegel and Novalis, from the cool, clear and transparent air of Protestantism into a foreign faith. The *leitmotiv* of Verlaine's poetry was his yearning and the infinitely beautiful and persistent impulse of the unhappy toward childhood and the magic of a primitively reverent life close to God. These wrought the miracle.

If trust were to be put in the corrupt man of letters who wrote the *Confessions*, it was a true miracle, like that in the cell of Saint Anthony, which brought him into the arms of the Church.

In his narrow room, in which he read Shakespeare and other worldly books, hung a simple crucifix, unnoticed at first. Of it he wrote:

"I know not what or Who suddenly raised me in the night, threw me from my bed without even leaving me time to dress, and prostrated me weeping and sobbing at the feet of the crucifix and before the supererogatory image of the Catholic Church, which has evoked the most strange, but in my eyes the most sublime devotion of modern times."

On the following day he asked for a priest and confessed his sins. At that hour, Verlaine, the Catholic poet, was born. He was wonderfully primitive, like the early poets of the Church, and his verses were as full of profound mystic poetry as those of the saints, Augustine and Francis of Assisi, and those of the German philosopher poets, Eckart and Tauler.

During these two years the neophyte wrote *Sagesse*, a volume which appeared later under the imprint of an exclusively Catholic publisher. It is the deepest and greatest work of French poetry, "the white crown of his work," Verhaeren calls it in his brilliant study of Verlaine. Here again, as once in the *Bonne Chanson*, the divergent forms of his character unite. In the unrestrained solution of everything personal in the divine, in "the melting of his own heart in the glowing heart of God," impulse and yearning are purified. Eroticism becomes spiritualized into fervor; hope, into sublime enlightenment; passion, devouring earthly dross, takes the form of mystic surrender. Thus the impulsive in Verlaine, permeated by hours of pure emotion, obtains its wild power of beauty, and trembles in the inexplicable mystery and in the stream of visionary light, so that his entire life now seems illumined.

In his religion likewise it is the purely human element which is so wonderful. Verlaine does not possess the seraphic mildness of Novalis, nor the consumptive, girl-like, sickly-beautiful inclination of the pre-Raphaelites toward the miraculous image. He is passionate and vehement. He is masculine where the others become feminine. Like a timid girl, Novalis dreams of Jesus as his bride. "If I have Him only, if He only is mine," he says and his words become a chaste love song.

Verlaine, however, is a reverberating echo of the great seekers after God, of the church fathers, of St. Augustine and of the mystics, and he wrestles for an almost physical love of God. His passion is often impious in its earthiness; his yearning, sacrilege.

In his sonnet cycle, *Mon dieu m'a dit*, is a place where the soul, wounded by the lighting of divine love, cries out, unconscious whether in joy or pain:

"Quoi, moi, moi pouvoir Vous aimer.
Êtes-vous fous?"

In these impious words God is humanized vividly, and yet, by the very bitterness of the struggle with His all-goodness, the poet imbues Him with an absolute perfection.

Here Verlaine's tormented soul is entirely cast out of himself, and plunges in a sudden flood into the infinite. Ecstasy overcomes the feminine element in him, just as in his life vulgar drunkenness roused his hard, coarse and brutal qualities. For a moment Verlaine is not only a genuine and marvellous, but also a truly strong and creative poet; no longer elegiac and sensitive, but creative.

In the reflux of enthusiasm come silent tender hours with songs in which the notes are muffled. They are the poems he wrote in the prison which gave him quietude and shelter, and in the silence of which the soft voices of his childhood rose again. Each one of these poems is noble, simple, and chaste. It is only necessary to name the titles to hear the soft violin note of their mild sadness – "Un grand sommeil noir," "Le ciel, est, par dessus le toit," "Je ne sais pas pourquoi mon esprit amer," "Le son du cor," "Je ne veux plus aimer que ma mère Marie."

It is truly "*le cœur plus veuf que toutes les veuves*" that speaks in them.

When the "*guote suendaere*" again went out into life which he had never been able to master, and the wild restlessness and

✻ 47

torment began which tore his heart into tatters, nothing remained of the two years in prison except his pious faith and a sorrowful memory. The four walls which had enclosed him also had protected him. "He was truly himself only in the hospital and in prison," says Huysmans.

Poor Lelian's longing plaint is for this silence. "Ah truly, I regret the two years in the tower." His song says "Formerly I dwelt in the best of castles." His yearning for the elemental, "far from a curbed age," never left him since those hours, and least of all in Paris, the city of his crowning fame as a poet. Faith he soon lost, but never the yearning for faith.

In addition Verlaine wrote a long series of Catholic poems. As will be shown later, he outraged his unique qualities and thus destroyed them. The unconscious portion, the wonderful fragrance of his early religious poems, which were entirely emotional, soon dissipated. He constructed an infinite number of pious verses, verses for saints' days, religious emblems, and compiled volumes of poetry for Catholic publishers. At the same time he edited pornographica and all manner of indecencies. His conversion had created a sensation. He had been thrust into a rôle and felt it his duty to play the part and to retain the costume. This was the reason for the antithesis. I do not believe the faith of his later years to have been genuine. He has called himself "the ruin of a still Christian philosopher already pagan," and in his obscene books turned the rites of Catholic faith, which he elsewhere glorified, into phallic and other sexual symbols.

He was unable to escape the realization of the comedy of this situation. In his autobiography, *Hommes d'aujourd'hui*, he attempted a very ingenious but exceedingly unsatisfactory justification. "His work," he explains, speaking of poor Lelian, "from 1880 took on two very sharply defined directions, and the prospectuses of his future books indicated that he had made up his mind to continue this system and to publish, if not simultaneously, at least in parallel, works absolutely different in idea – to be more exact, books in which Catholicism unfolds its logic and its lures, its blandishments and its terrors; and others purely modern, sensual with a distressing good humor and full of the pride of life."

Can this be the program of the "unconscious?"

A few lines further on he has given another explanation. "I believe, and I am a good Christian at this moment; I believe, and I am a bad Christian the instant after. The remembrance of hope, the evocation of a sin, delight me with or without remorse." This is the truth. Verlaine was a man of moods, he was always only the creature of the moment. After a few seconds the movement of his will contracted limply and momentary desires overflooded his consciousness of personality. His faith may have been as capricious and restless, as each one of his tendencies of passion. Great poems, however, in the sense of great in extent, are not conceived in a moment. Moods spread like a fine mist over the poet's hours, they permeate them and fill them through and through for a long time before a poem takes form.

Verlaine, the man of letters and poet according to program, is a hateful shadow limping behind his great works. Consciously and with feverish eagerness and a productivity forced by need, he rhymed in what he thought his unique manner. The poor old man whom interviewers sought in the hospital was no longer the poet, Paul Verlaine.

It is impossible to tell how long the flame of personal faith still glowed in him. Probably it was as little extinguished as his soft dream of childhood. In the dusk of his last years it often struggled upward with tears, as a symbol of sorrow over his broken life.

As all his thought began to tend toward senile mistiness, his emotions also slowly deteriorated in indifference and drunken- ness. It was not his companions in his cups who understood him best, but the poets who saw his life in the illuminating perspective of distance.

In a short story, *Gestas*, Anatole France has marvellously described in his insistent, quiet, dignified fashion the mingling of purity and depravity in this life of curious piety. It is merely an anecdote. Stumbling, a drunkard enters church in the early morn to confess his sins. The priest has not yet arrived. The drunkard begins to grow noisy, beats the prayer desks; he rages and weeps, he has so endlessly many sins to confess, he wants only a little priest, a very, very little one.

In these few pages everything is compressed, "the prodigal child with the gestures of a satyr." All the traits of Verlaine are here, the accusing one of the penitent which he never lost, the angry one of the drunkard, the yearning tenderness of the poet, all the childishly wise, and yet in its simplicity so marvellously wonderful, faith of the good sinner.

LEGENDS AND LITERATURE

One hesitates to relate the last years of this curious life. From the moment that Verlaine returned to Paris the tragedy lacks æsthetic significance. There are no longer sudden descents and elevations, but his life is slowly stifled in *camaraderie*, lingering disease and depravity. His poetic force crumbles away, his uniqueness becomes extinguished. It is no longer a foaming wave crest that carries him away, but dirty little waves.

When he came to Paris, he had been forgotten. His books were lying unsold with the publishers; the majority of his friends avoided him, evidently because their frock coat of the Academy made recognition difficult, until suddenly the younger generation began to noise about his name; and now more people quarrel over starting this movement than there were cities to claim Homer's cradle.

It was a period of development. French lyric poetry was passing through a revolutionary crisis. For the first time the marble image of *"beauté impassible"* trembled in the hands of the poets. But not one of them was a strong enough artist to create a new ideal. At this moment the younger men began to remember Verlaine. His Bohemian life, the soft, fluctuating dreamy manner of his art, the frenzy of his life, his recklessness, loyalty and elementalness were a marvellous antithesis to the well-bred *"impassibilité"* of the Academy. His name was used as a battering-ram against the Parnassians. In kindly fashion, without choice, Verlaine, the old man, who was beginning to feel chill, accepted the late enthusiasm and veneration.

Literature alone is not yet sufficient to create fame in France. It was only when the great journals began to take an interest in his life that he became popular. And at that time a mass of paltry legends began to gather around his name. He became the "naive child of modern culture," the "Bohemian," the "Unconscious," the "New François Villon," and even to-day these stereotyped phrases are industriously repeated.

Indeed his life was strange. In hospitals the poet sought shelter. With a white cloth wound like a turban around his bald, Socrates-like head, he was always surrounded by contemporary literature, which strove to rise with the aid of his name. He received interviewers, and wrote his poems on prescription blanks and smeary tatters. When he was well, he wandered from café to café, holding forth and gesticulating, getting drunk, and associating with lewd women, always with a certain ostentation whenever he noticed that the public was watching him. As a senile Silenus, he presided over the most remarkable bacchanalia. Like a second Victor Hugo, he patronized the younger men with benevolent gesture. A forced merriness seemed in those days to tremble electrically through his nerves. Yet never before had his life been filled with deeper tragedy and yearning, and there were many hours when he himself felt this keenly. Crushed and torn by the teeth of life, he, like all Bohemians, at last desired only peace. Never was the sweet dream of his childhood days more poignant than in just this period of dissolute play-acting and vain exhibitionism.

Taine has very accurately shown that creative art consists in the automatization of the creative individuality, in overhearing and imitating inherent qualities, and in objectifying the personal elements. This process too became operative in Verlaine's life, more markedly because in him life and personality were immanent interaction.

He caricatured himself and re-drew the delicate lines of his soul with crude pencil. Consciously he tried to make the unconscious elements take plastic form again by way of reflection. He was no longer elemental, but he strove hard to be. He prayed to God "to give me all simplicity," because he knew it was expected of him. Since he was counted among the Catholic poets, he tried again to pass through the storm of sacred emotion. The effort resulted in pompous, well-constructed religious poems, plump like botched Roman churches.

He attempted to show the unconscious in himself by striving to explain the creative impulse and placing mirrors behind his juggler's tricks. The wonderful gesture of surrender which destiny and sorrow had taught him, he learned by heart like an actor who reproduces a gesture mechanically at the seventy succeeding performances, though he is truly an artist only at the moment when he first discovers and understands its significance in studying the part. Thus Verlaine carefully reconstructed all the characteristics which the journals declared were his own. Coquettishly he exhibited the "poor Lelian" and the *"bon enfant"* – mere costumes of a poetical fire that had long died out. His manner became more and more childlike; he was trying to enter entirely into the rôle of *"guileless fool,"* while his sharp but unlogical intelligence never gave way.

The poet retired further and further into him. The more he rhymed (and in the last years with morbid frequency), the fewer poems were produced. Now and then one came, when pose and impulse joined in minutes of sad (or drunken) melancholy, and when the mysterious fluid of the unconscious and great indefinite emotions made him silent, simple and timid.

Otherwise he alternately turned erotic incidents and adventures in alcoves into rhyme, and wrote literary mockeries and parodies of Paul Verlaine, and for purposes of contrast, verses in praise of Catholic saint days. Every artistic pride was soon forgotten in the need for money. He sold his poems at one hundred sous apiece to his publisher Vanier, who cruelly printed them often against the active protest of the poet; recently again a volume of "Posthumous Works," which easily may be denominated as one of the most disagreeable and worst books published in France. This portion of the tragedy of his life no one has as yet fully told.

During his last years he wrote two books which must not be ignored even though they do not fit in the customary picture of the *bon enfant*. These were *Femmes* and *Hombres*. They could not appear publicly but were sold in five hundred numbered copies each. In them Verlaine broke abruptly with the tradition of agreeable nastiness of a Grecourt, in order to produce works of an unheard-of subjective shamelessness. In form the poems are smooth and in structure they are clever, but their subject matter and the poet's self-revelation is such as to place these volumes among the most unhappy that have ever been produced. They are naked and obscene.

From an æsthetic point of view this publication, even if it was clandestine was without excuse, and it was the deepest descent of the poet. The effect of this depravity of an old man writing down with unsteady hand vices and nakednesses on prescription blanks for the sake of a few francs with which to buy an absinthe, is tragic. The existence and the spread of these books must destroy absolutely the legend of the "guileless fool." This is the only value which can be attributed to them.

The carnival comedy took place before Ash Wednesday. When Leconte de Lisle died, the younger generation advertised and arranged for the choice of the king of poets, never realizing to what extent they were guilty in bringing about the artistic degeneration of the chosen poet. The faun-like, mockingly sagacious head of Paul Verlaine, who was ill and growing old, received the crown. Poor Lelian became "king of the poets," a mark of great affection on the part of the younger men, but only a title after all, which was unable to give Paul Verlaine the necessary dignity and strength of personality. After Verlaine, Stéphane Mallarmé inherited the imaginary crown, and after him it was worn in obscurity by Leon Dierx,[3] a not very distinguished, but agreeable and dignified poet of the former Parnassus. The coronation was only a pose and voluntary choice, and would hardly be worth considering were it not for the fact that this admiration for Verlaine's work indicated an underlying tendency in modern French poetry.

To the younger generation Verlaine represented not only a great poet, but to them he was also the regenerator of French lyric poetry. The legend that Verlaine consciously changed poetic valuations is entirely due to a single poem, the "*Art Poétique*." It is absolutely necessary to quote it, because on the one hand it is characteristic of Verlaine's instinct concerning his own work, and because on the other hand it is the basis of all the formulas which became dogmas among the verse jugglers.

> "De la musique avant toute chose,
> Et pour cela préfère l'Impair
> Plus vague et plus soluble dans l'air,
> Sans rien en lui, qui pèse ou qui pose.
> "Il faut aussi que tu n'ailles point
> Choisir tes mots sans quelque méprise:
> Rien de plus cher que la chanson grise
> Où l'Indécis au Précis se joint.
>
> "C'est des beaux yeux derrière les voiles,
> C'est le grand jour tremblant de midi,
> C'est, par un ciel d'automne attiédi,
> Le bleu fouillis des claires étoiles!
> "Car nous voulons la Nuance encore,
> Pas la Couleur, rien que la nuance!
> Oh, la nuance seule fiance
> Le rêve au rêve et la flûte au cor!
> "Fuis du plus loin la Pointe assassine,
> L'Esprit cruel et le Rire impur,
> Qui font pleurer les yeux d'Azur
> Et tout cet ail de basse cuisine!
> "Prends l'éloquence et tords-lui son cou!
> Tu feras bien, en train d'énergie,
> De rendre un peu la Rime assagie,
> Si l'on n'y veille, elle ira jusqu'où?

"Oh! qui dira les torts de la Rime?
Quel enfant sourd ou quel nègre fou
Nous a forgé ce bijou d'un sou
Qui sonne creux et faux sous la lime?
"De la musique encore et toujours!
Que ton vers soit la chose envolée
Qu'on sent qui fuit d'une âme en allée
Vers d'autres cieux à d'autres amours.

"Que ton vers soit la bonne aventure
Éparse au vent crispé du matin
Qui va fleurant la menthe et le thym ...
Et tout le reste est littérature."

(ART POÉTIQUE

No laws should rule by force or guile,
But let your verse go singing soft,
And in the solvent air aloft
Find music, music all the while.
Nor be too diffident in phrase,
But let your song grow drunk with wine
Where mystic unions vaguely shine
In luminous and errant ways.
Like veilèd eyes your song should be,
Like noondays trembling in the sun,
Like autumn dusks when days are done
And stars and sky join secretly.
Not vivid colors should adorn,
But shades alone when dream to dream
Is wed, and tender shadows gleam
Like flute notes mingled with the horn.
The "point" which slays and cruel wit,
And smile impure you should despise,
For like base garlic they arise
To spoil the poem exquisite.

Take eloquence and twist its neck!
And sophist rhyming which would lead
You headlong into sing-song speed
'Tis well for you to hold in check.
Oh, who shall tell of evil rhyme!
A trinket coin with hollow ring,
A barbarous or childish thing

Passed downward idly to our time.
Music, music, evermore,
The burden of your song should be,
Inherent like the melody
Of souls a-wing to distant shore;
Or like the brave emprise and pure
Of morning breezes which imbue
The thyme and mint with honey dew –
The rest belongs to literature).

Without question certain words in these lines, somewhat veiled by the poetic form of expression, harmonize with the fundamental conceptions of modern impressionistic lyric poetry. France never was the land of pure emotional poetry. There is too much sense of the formal, too much of a keen-sighted almost mathematical type of intellect mingled with a gallant pleasure in pointedness among the French, and these make them turn into logic the elements of mysticism which must be in every poem, whether in its emotional content or its vague form of expression. Goethe has proclaimed the incommensurable as the material of all poetry, but among the French the tendency to crystallize it in the solution of their positivist habit of thought is ever imperceptibly betrayed. The feeling for the line and style shows through. For them poetry is architecture; intuition, their intellectual formula; the marble of conceptions is their material, and rhyme the mortar.

Clarity and orderly arrangement are the preliminary conditions for Victor Hugo, for the Parnassians and even for Baudelaire, even though the latter, by his visionary form and the opiate of his dark words, created for the first time solemn, that is to say poetical, impressions instead of those of pomp alone. It seems therefore an error to look for the revolutionary tendency and literary importance of a Verlaine in the looseness of his verse structure and more careless (or intentionally careless) use of rhyme. His merit is rather that he was able to illume chaos, darkness, and presentiments by the very indefiniteness and the vague music of his soul. This enabled him to endue his poems with their mystical trembling melody, not by abstracting his inner music in definite melodies, but by fixing it in assonance, rhymes and rhythmic waves.

Unconsciously he recognized that lyric art is the most immaterial of all and is most nearly related to music. Its aërial trembling and immateriality may meet the soul in waves of glowing fire, but intellectually it is unseizable. He tried to preserve this musical element by means of harmony and assonance, but it was not he himself so much as the unconscious gift of poetry that played mysteriously in him and made him find the fundamental secret of lyric effects. Émile Verhaeren, the only other French poet who is a more vehement and constructive character, sought and found the musical element of lyric poetry by the only other way, that is, in verbal rhythm or consonantal music. Thus to volatilize the material simultaneously in the form and to join the technical with the intuitive elements is the highest quality of lyric poetry. It makes it immediate, organic, that is to say, its spiritual elements permeate the material in immanent reaction, and thus the mystery of life is renewed in individual artifacts. Self-evidently this intuitive recognition is no discovery. It has been present in the great lyric poets of all time, a mystery like that of sexual reproduction, which awakens only at the age of ripeness. It was new in France only because, besides Villon, Verlaine was the first lyric genius of the French.

The mystery of the German folk-song with its simple, sweetly mysterious essence became realized in him, perhaps because there was an undercurrent of national relationship. Because of the weakness, submissiveness and child-like confusion of his emotion- ality, the vibrations became tonality, sound and, because he was a poet, music, instead of intellectual structures.

Such art must be more effective as contrasted with all intellectualism because it springs from deeper sources, just as simple weeping is more eloquent than passionate wailing aloud. Surely it also contains an artificial element, not artistry, but magic art, or the "alchemy of the word" which Rimbaud believed to have discovered, a relationship between colors, vowels and sounds depending on idiosyncrasy. It is a secret touching of the ultimate roots of different stems. It is always necessary to assume an inter-relation between lyricism and the lawless, enigmatic and magic elements of the human soul and to associate vague threshold emotions with soft music.

Verlaine's poetry during his creative period possesses this vagueness, which is like a voice in the dark or music of the soul. It also has the lack of coherence which emotions must have when they sweep in halting pain through the body. This element must remain incomprehensible to commercially sharp intelligences of the type of Max Nordau, who try in a way to subtract the net value of purely intellectual elements and "contents" which could be reduced to prose from the gross value of poems. Lyricism is magic and the precious possession of a spiritual communion which finds its deepest enjoyment in just these almost impalpable elements.

To limit the most important element of Verlaine's significance to his neglect of rhyme is showing poor judgment. In the first place it is unimportant and secondly incorrect, for he never wrote a poem without rhyme, except in the later unworthy years, when now and then he substituted assonances. In addition he has himself protested in *L'Hommes d'Aujourd'hui*:

> "In the past and at present too I am honored by having my name mingled with these disputes, and I pass for a bitter adversary of rhyme because of a selection published in a recent collection. – Besides absolute liberty is my device if it were necessary for me to have one – and I find good everything which is good in despite and notwithstanding rules."

To many it was insufficient to celebrate Verlaine as one of the marvels of a nation, a truly elemental human being whose soul uttered the finest and most tender lyric moods and who, as if awakened out of bell-like and clear dreams, produced true and melodic poetry out of the darkness of his life. His admirers have also praised him as a prose writer. But the prose-writer must be an intellectual creator, and know how to master form. This Verlaine was unable to do. He never really understood the world, and knew only how to tell of himself, and accordingly his novelettes are for the most part concealed autobiographies. They have brilliant portions of characterization. His intellect, which is paradoxical, self-willed, lyrical, and abrupt, flashes up and then crumbles.

His *Confessions*, which have been highly praised, remind one of Rousseau's all too confidential and hypocritical confessions. They are only documents of personal sharp-sightedness, unfortunately much over-clouded by literary pose. He also tried the theatre. His comedy, *Les Uns et les Autres*, has Watteau-like style and Pierrot elegances, as well as flexibility, but is of no importance. Another play, *Louis XVI*, remained a fragment. All Verlaine's literary productions, like biographies, introductions, etc., give a painful impression because they are forced and have sprung from evil *camaraderie.*

He has also been called a great draftsman. It is true that an excellent and characteristic skill in the figures and scribblings which he sprinkled throughout his letters cannot be gainsaid. There is even a pathetic element in their self-confessed technical imperfections. The caricatures are playful, without malicious or serious intent, jotted down with childish self-satisfaction, but, of course, they need not be taken seriously. They are little marginalia to his life, and addenda to the numerous sharp and bright sketches with which his intimate friend and artistic Eckermann, F. A. Cazals, has fixed him for posterity. They show Verlaine in all his moods – in his bonhomie, despair, grief, "*gaminerie*," sexuality, disease, even to the last sketches which show him in death. They form a gallery of his life from childhood to childhood along the dark way of his destiny. And as in his poetry, notwithstanding all the exuberant passages, the final impression is a wailing note of sadness – the stroke of melancholy's bow.

POSTLUDE

The only thing which now remains is to ascertain whether Paul Verlaine's life-work, beginning in Metz and ending in a small lodging-house room in Paris on a January day in 1896, contains the elements which we would call "lasting" because we are afraid of the proud and resounding word "eternal." The significance of great poets passes the boundaries of literature and ignores what is known as "influences" and "artistic atmosphere." The eternal element of great works of poetry reaches back toward eternity. For humanity poetry is infinity which it joins with the ether, and the great poets are those who were able to help in elaborating the wonderful bond which stretches from the distant darkness to the red of the new dawn.

It does not diminish Verlaine's stature if we do not count him among the heroes of life. He was an isolated phenomena, too significant to be typical and too weak to become eternal. There was beauty in his pure humanness, but not of the kind which remains permanent. He has given nothing which was not already in us. He was a fleeting stream of life passing by; he was the sublime echo of the mysterious music which rises within us on every contact of things, like the ring of glasses on a cupboard under every footstep and impact.

His effect is deep, but yet on that account not great. To have become great it would have been necessary for him to conquer the destiny which he could not master and to liberate his will from the thousand little vices and passions which enwrapped it. He is one of the writers who could be spared, whom nevertheless no one would do without. He is a marvel, beautiful and unnecessary, like a rare flower which gives sweetness and wonderful peace to the senses, but which does not make us noble, strong, brave and humble.

He was, and herein lies his greatness and power, the symbol of pure humanity, splendid creative force in the weak vessel of his personality. He was a poet who in his works became one with the poetry of life, the sounds of the forest, the kiss of the wind, the rustling of the reeds and the voice of the dusk of evening. Humanly he was like us who love him. He was one of those who, no matter how great a chaos they have made of their own life, are yet inappeasable, and drink the stranger's pain and the stranger's bliss in the precious cup of glorious poetry. They manifold their being and their emotions because of a blind and uncreative yearning for the universal and infinity.

FOOTNOTES

1. In French *Pauvre Lelian*, an anagram of Paul Verlaine, which Verlaine often used when speaking of himself.
2. A Biography and a volume of Rimbaud's correspondence have recently been published by his brother-in-law, Paterne Berrichon. They throw much light upon his remarkable career.
3. Leon Dierx died in 1912 at the age of 74, and Paul Fort, the author of the famous *Ballades Françaises*, was chosen as "king of the poets" to succeed him.

POEMS BY PAUL VERLAINE

Translated by Arthur Symons

CLAIR DE LUNE

Votre âme est un paysage choisi
Que vont charmants masques et bergamasques,
Jouant du luth et dansant et quasi
Tristes sous leurs déguisements fantasques.

Tout en chantant sur le mode mineur
L'amour vainqueur et la vie opportune,
Ils n'ont pas l'air de croire à leur bonheur
Et leur chanson se mêle au clair de lune,

Au calme clair de lune triste et beau,
Qui fait rêver les oiseaux dans les arbres
Et sangloter d'extase les jets d'eau,
Les grands jets d'eau sveltes parmi les marbres.

CLAIR DE LUNE

Your soul is a sealed garden, and there go
With masque and bergamasque fair companies
Playing on lutes and dancing and as though
Sad under their fantastic fripperies.

Though they in minor keys go carolling
Of love the conqueror and of life the boon
They seem to doubt the happiness they sing
And the song melts into the light of the moon,

The sad light of the moon, so lovely fair
That all the birds dream in the leafy shade
And the slim fountains sob into the air
Among the marble statues in the glade.

CHANSON D'AUTOMNE

Les sanglots longs
Des violons
    De l'automne
Blessent mon coeur
D'une langueur
    Monotone.

Tout suffocant
Et blême, quand
    Sonne l'heure,
Je me souviens
Des jours anciens
    Et je pleure;

Et je m'en vais
Au vent mauvais
    Qui m'emporte
Deçà, delà,
Pareil à la
    Feuille morte.

CHANSON D'AUTOMNE

When a sighing begins
In the violins
Of the autumn-song,
My heart is drowned
In the slow sound
Languorous and long.

Pale as with pain,
Breath fails me when
The hour tolls deep.
My thoughts recover
The days that are over,
And I weep.

And I go

Where the winds know,
Broken and brief,
To and fro,
As the winds blow
A dead leaf.

"C'EST L'EXTASE LANGOUREUSE"

C'est l'extase langoureuse,
C'est la fatigue amoureuse,
C'est tous les frissons des bois
Parmi l'étreinte des brises,
C'est, vers les ramures grises,
Le choeur des petites voix.

O le frêle et frais murmure!
Cela gazouille et susure,
Cela ressemble au cri doux
Que l'herbe agitée expire...
Tu dirais, sous l'eau qui vire,
Le roulis sourd des cailloux.

Cette âme qui se lamente
En cette plainte dormante,
C'est la nôtre, n'est-ce pas?
La mienne, dis, et la tienne,
Dont s'exhale l'humble antienne
Par ce tiède soir, tout bas?

"C'EST L'EXTASE LANGOUREUSE"

'Tis the ecstasy of repose,
'Tis love when tired lids close,
'Tis the wood's long shuddering
In the embrace of the wind,
'Tis, where grey boughs are thinned,
Little voices that sing.

O fresh and frail is the sound
That twitters above, around,
Like the sweet tiny sigh
That lies in the shaken grass;
Or the sound when waters pass
And the pebbles shrink and cry.

What soul is this that complains
Over the sleeping plains,
And what is it that it saith?
Is it mine, is it thine,
This lowly hymn I divine
In the warm night, low as a breath?

MANDOLINE

Les donneurs de sérénades
Et les belles écouteuses
Échangent des propos fades
Sous les ramures chanteuses.

C'est Tircis et c'est Aminte,
Et c'est l'éternel Clitandre,
Et c'est Damis qui pour mainte
Cruelle fait maint vers tendre.

Leurs courtes vestes de soie,
Leurs longues robes à queues,
Leur élégance, leur joie
Et leurs molles ombres bleues,

Tourbillonnent dans l'extase
D'une lune rose et grise,
Et la mandoline jase
Parmi les frissons de brise.

MANDOLINE

The singers of serenades
Whisper their faded vows
Unto fair listening maids
Under the singing boughs.

Tircis, Aminte, are there,
Clitandre has waited long,
And Damis for many a fair
Tyrant makes many a song.

Their short vests, silken and bright,
Their long pale silken trains,
Their elegance of delight,
Twine soft blue silken chains.

And the mandolines and they,
Faintlier breathing, swoon
Into the rose and grey
Ecstasy of the moon.

A CLYMÈNE

Mystiques barcarolles,
Romances sans paroles,
Chère, puisque tes yeux,
Couleur des cieux,

Puisque ta voix, étrange
Vision qui dérange
Et trouble l'horizon
De ma raison,

Puisque l'arôme insigne
De ta pâleur de cygne
Et puisque la candeur
De ton odeur,

Ah! puisque tout ton être,
Musique qui pénètre,
Nimbes d'anges défunts,
Tons et parfums.

A sur d'almes cadences
En ses correspondances,
Induit mon coeur subtil,
Ainsi soit-il!

A CLYMÈNE

Mystical strains unheard,
A song without a word,
Dearest, because thine eyes,
Pale as the skies,

Because thy voice, remote
As the far clouds that float
Veiling for me the whole
Heaven of the soul,

Because the stately scent
Of thy swan's whiteness, blent
With the white lily's bloom
Of thy perfume,

Ah! because thy dear love,
The music breathed above
By angels halo-crowned,
Odour and sound,

Hath, in my subtle heart,
With some mysterious art
Transposed thy harmony,
So let it be!

COLOMBINE

Léandre le sot,
Pierrot qui d'un saut
De puce
Franchit le buisson,
Cassandre sous son
Capuce,

Arlequin aussi,
Cet aigrefin si
Fantasque
Aux costumes fous,
Ses yeux luisants sous
Son masque,

– Do, mi, sol, mi, fa, –
Tout ce monde va,
Rit, chante
Et danse devant
Une belle enfant
Méchante

Dont les yeux pervers
Comme les yeux verts
Des chattes
Gardent ses appas
Et disent: «A bas
Les pattes!»

– Eux ils vont toujours!
Fatidique cours
Des astres,
Oh! dis-moi vers quels

Mornes ou cruels
Désastres

L'implacable enfant,
Preste et relevant
Ses jupes,
La rose au chapeau,
Conduit son troupeau
De dupes?

COLUMBINE

The foolish Leander,
Cape-covered Cassander,
And which
Is Pierrot? 'tis he
With the hop of a flea
Leaps the ditch;

And Harlequin who
Rehearses anew
His sly task,
With his dress that's a wonder,
And eyes shining under
His mask;

Mi, sol, mi, fa, do!
How gaily they go,
And they sing
And they laugh and they twirl
Round the feet of a girl
Like the Spring,

Whose eyes are as green
As a cat's are, and keen
As its claws,
And her eyes without frown
Bid all new-comers Down
With your paws!

On they go with the force
Of the stars in their course,
And the speed:
O tell me toward what

Disaster unthought,
Without heed

The implacable fair,
A rose in her hair,
Holding up
Her skirts as she runs
Leads this dance of the dunce
And the dupe?

"LA LAUNE BLANCHE"

La lune blanche
Luit dans les bois;
De chaque branche
Part une voix
Sous la ramée…

O bien-aimée.

L'étang reflète,
Profond miroir,
La silhouette
Du saule noir
Où le vent pleure…

Rêvons, c'est l'heure.

Un vaste et tendre
Apaisement
Semble descendre
Du firmament
Que l'astre irise…

C'est l'heure exquise.

"LA LAUNE BLANCHE"

The white moon sits
And seems to brood
Where a swift voice flits
From each branch in the wood
That the tree-tops cover....

O lover, my lover!

The pool in the meadows
Like a looking-glass
Casts back the shadows
That over it pass
Of the willow-bower....

Let us dream: 'tis the hour....

A tender and vast
Lull of content
Like a cloud is cast
From the firmament
Where one planet is bright....

'Tis the hour of delight.

"IL PLEURE DANS MON COEUR"

Il pleut doucement sur la ville.
(ARTHUR RAIMBAUD.)

Il pleure dans mon coeur
Comme il pleut sur la ville,
Quelle est cette langueur
Qui pénètre mon coeur?

O bruit doux de la pluie
Par terre et sur les toits!
Pour un coeur qui s'ennuie,
O le chant de la pluie!

Il pleure sans raison
Dans ce coeur qui s'écoeure.
Quoi! nulle trahison?
Ce deuil est sans raison.

C'est bien la pire peine
De ne savoir pourquoi,
Sans amour et sans haine,
Mon coeur a tant de peine!

"IL PLEURE DANS MON COEUR"

Tears in my heart that weeps,
Like the rain upon the town.
What drowsy languor steeps
In tears my heart that weeps?

O sweet sound of the rain
On earth and on the roofs!
For a heart's weary pain
O the song of the rain!

Vain tears, vain tears, my heart!
What, none hath done thee wrong?
Tears without reason start
From my disheartened heart.

This is the weariest woe,
O heart, of love and hate
Too weary, not to know
Why thou hast all this woe.

SPLEEN

Les roses étaient toutes rouges,
Et les lierres étaient tout noirs.
Chère, pour peu que tu te bouges,
Renaissent tous mes désespoirs.

Le ciel était trop bleu, trop tendre,
La mer trop verte et l'air trop doux.
Je crains toujours, – ce qu'est d'attendre
Quelque fuite atroce de vous.

Du houx à la feuille vernie
Et du luisant buis je suis las,
Et de la campagne infinie
Et de tout, fors de vous, hélas!

SPLEEN

The roses were all red,
The ivy was all black:
Dear, if you turn your head,
All my despairs come back.

The sky was too blue, too kind,
The sea too green, and the air
Too calm: and I know in my mind
I shall wake and not find you there.

I am tired of the box-tree's shine
And the holly's, that never will pass,
And the plain's unending line,
And of all but you, alas!

ART POÉTIQUE

A Charles Morice.

De la musique avant toute chose,
Et pour cela préfère l'Impair
Plus vague et plus soluble dans l'air,
Sans rien en lui qui pèse ou qui pose.

Il faut aussi que tu n'ailles point
Choisir tes mots sans quelque méprise:
Rien de plus cher que la chanson grise
Où l'Indécis au Précis se joint.

C'est des beaux yeux derrière les voiles,
C'est le grand jour tremblant de midi,
C'est, par un ciel d'automne attiédi,
Le bleu fouillis des claires étoiles!

Car nous voulons la Nuance encor,
Pas la Couleur, rien que la nuance!
Oh! la nuance seule fiance
Le rêve au rêve et la flûte au cor!

Fuis du plus loin la Pointe assassine,
L'Esprit cruel et le rire impur,
Qui font pleurer les yeux de l'Azur,
Et tout cet ail de basse cuisine!

Prends l'éloquence et tords-lui son cou!
Tu feras bien, en train d'énergie,
De rendre un peu la Rime assagie.
Si l'on n'y veille, elle ira jusqu'où?

O qui dira les torts de la Rime!
Quel enfant sourd ou quel nègre fou
Nous a forgé ce bijou d'un sou
Qui sonne creux et faux sous la lime?

De la musique encore et toujours!
Que ton vers soit la chose envolée
Qu'on sent qui fuit d'une âme en allée
Vers d'autres cieux à d'autres amours.

Que ton vers soit la bonne aventure
Éparse au vent crispé du matin
Qui va fleurant la menthe et le thym…
Et tout le reste est littérature.

ART POÉTIQUE

Music first and foremost of all!
Choose your measure of odd not even,
Let it melt in the air of heaven,
Pose not, poise not, but rise and fall.

Choose your words, but think not whether
Each to other of old belong:
What so dear as the dim grey song
Where clear and vague are joined together?

'Tis veils of beauty for beautiful eyes,
'Tis the trembling light of the naked noon,
'Tis a medley of blue and gold, the moon
And stars in the cool of autumn skies.

Let every shape of its shade be born;
Colour, away! come to me, shade!
Only of shade can the marriage be made
Of dream with dream and of flute with horn.

Shun the Point, lest death with it come,
Unholy laughter and cruel wit
(For the eyes of the angels weep at it)
And all the garbage of scullery-scum.

Take Eloquence, and wring the neck of him!
You had better, by force, from time to time,
Put a little sense in the head of Rhyme:
If you watch him not, you will be at the beck of him.

O, who shall tell us the wrongs of Rhyme?
What witless savage or what deaf boy

✳ 90

Has made for us this twopenny toy
Whose bells ring hollow and out of time?

Music always and music still!
Let your verse be the wandering thing
That flutters in flight from a soul on the wing
Towards other skies at a new whim's will.

Let your verse be the luck of the lure
Afloat on the winds that at morning hint
Of the odours of thyme and the savour of mint …
And all the rest is literature.

Henri Fantin-Latour, The Corner of the Table, 1872,
Musée d'Orsay, Paris

A NOTE ON PAUL VERLAINE

By Andrew Jary

Paul Verlaine (1844-1896) is one of the great 19th century French poets, part of the group that included Charles Baudelaire, Lautréamont, Gérard de Nerval and of course Arthur Rimbaud. Many of Verlaine's most significant poems are collected in this book, and Verlaine emerges as a highly accomplished artist, with a lyrical rhyming style that's wholly his own (and it sounds particularly beautiful in French – Verlaine is tricky to translate).

Paul Verlaine's era was that of Symbolism and Decadence, and the chief poets of Symbolism and Decadence included Verlaine, Charles Baudelaire, Arthur Rimbaud, Gérard de Nerval, Tristan Corbière, Stéphane Mallarmé, Paul Valéry and Lautréamont. The Symbolist and Decadent age is marked by 'gory exoticism', as Mario Praz put it (289), by the æstheticism of 'beauty', opulence and indulgence, mysticism and black magic, the macabre, where the key phrase is from Paul Verlaine: 'Je suis l'Empire à la fin de la décadence', which he wrote in 1885 in a poem entitled (what else?) 'Langueur'.[1] The word, *decadence*, from Verlaine, connotes profuse amounts of eroticism, debauchery, declining state power, Imperialism and 'perversions'.

Like other poets of the Symbolist era – Arthur Rimbaud,

---

1 P. Verlaine, 1999, 134.

Stéphane Mallarmé, Banville – Paul Verlaine can be seen as post-Romantic. Verlaine's poetry (like Symbolism) exhibits many affinities with Romanticism: the pantheism and nature mysticism; the love of occultism, paganism, Hellenism, travel and exotica; the cult of the individual; the social rebellion; the exaltation of solitude; the sense of melancholy; the emphasis on subjective experience; the use of drugs and intoxicants; the urge to go to extremes; the leaning towards infinity, and so on.

Paul Verlaine was an important poet, but was not epoch-forming like Arthur Rimbaud, Victor Hugo or Charles Baudelaire. Verlaine's poetry is marked by a finely-crafted musicality and sense of form, a delicate sensuality, and large doses of Catholic imagery and religious themes.

Paul Verlaine's emphasis in poetry on the form, precision, musicality and beauty of poetry contrasted dramatically with the sense of burning abandon in poets such as Rimbaud, de Nerval and Lautréamont. There is a wildness in Arthur Rimbaud's poetic sensibility that no poetic form can quite contain (despite his use of many traditional forms). While Verlaine's poetry remains firmly within the form of the stanza, Rimbaud's threatens to burst out. What Rimbaud and Verlaine share, with poets such as Baudelaire, William Blake, Novalis and Friedrich Hölderlin, is a belief in the magic of poetry. Theirs is a poetics of the word, an 'alchemy of the word'. as Rimbaud put it.

Paul Verlaine developed Gérard de Nerval's mythopoeic brand of poetry, but for Verlaine form was crucial. 'Music before everything', he wrote in his influential poem 'Art poétique' (1974, 172-3). Verlaine's delicate poetic musicality was highly refined even in his first volume of verse, *Poèmes saturniens*. A poem such as 'Cansons d'automne' displays the finesse of Verlaine's sense of sound and music in poetry (it's also an important poem for France politically):

Les sanglots longs
Des violons

De l'automne
Blessent mon cœur
D'une langueur
    Monotone.
(The long sobbing of the violins of autumn wounds my heart with a
monotonous languour [1974, 44])

VERLAINE AND RIMBAUD

It is significant that the main documents relating to the relation-
ship between Paul Verlaine and Arthur Rimbaud is their poetry.[2]
Poetry is a very particular kind of creation, often having an
obscure or distant link to the poet's life or experience (involving
layers and veils of stylization and mythicization). Consequently,
using Verlaine's and Rimbaud's poems of the period or later
poetry to find out about their years together is fraught with
problems.

Paul Verlaine was ten years older than Arthur Rimbaud. Next
to the phenomenally talented teenage poet, Verlaine must have
felt inadequate. By an early age Rimbaud had already attained
everything that Verlaine had, artistically, and had far surpassed
him. The elements of their time together have become famous –
the arguments, the dissolute life in Northern Europe (including
Paris and London), and the incident with the gun, when Verlaine
shot Rimbaud during an argument.

Before he met Paul Verlaine, Arthur Rimbaud admired his
poetry. In his 'seer letter' of May 15, 1871, Rimbaud re-writes the
history of poetry. It is all junk, he claims, from the Greeks to the
Romantics (*Collected Works*, 305). Among the few poets to get a
favourable mention by the young Rimbaud are the Parnassians
Albert Mérat and Paul Verlaine (ib., 307).

2 W. Fowlie, 1995, 52.

Critics generally portray Paul Verlaine as the weaker, more feminine partner in their homosexual relationship, with Arthur Rimbaud as the more aggressive, more cynical partner. Rimbaud seemed to care much less about the relationship and about himself than Verlaine did. He certainly cared much less about art. It was Verlaine who tried to patch up the relationship after an interval apart. But both men had similar temperaments – too similar; both men were prone to violent mood swings; both were highly individual, self-opinionated, egotistic, unwilling to com-promise. They seemed well suited to each other, and yet, as events proved, ultimately incompatible.

Critics turn to Arthur Rimbaud's *A Season in Hell* (1873) as an account of aspects of the Verlaine-Rimbaud relationship: parts of *A Season In Hell* are intense, heartfelt, ashamed, vitriolic, unrepent-ant, transgressive, chaotic, stupid and sometimes violent. The first 'Delirium' poem is particularly visceral in its imagery, and intense in its self-examination.

Whether or not 'Delirium I: The Foolish Virgin' is an account of Arthur Rimbaud's time with Paul Verlaine, it certainly contains some of Rimbaud's most vivid and tortured poetry. Right from the start of 'Delirium I' the narrator or confessor is talking in extreme terms of being drunk, lost and impure. The confessor says that there has never been 'deliriums and tortures like this'. The confessor says he is really suffering. He speaks of the damned and the dead, of ghosts and murder, of treasure being stained with blood, of skeletons and throats being cut ('it'll be "disgusting"'). The Infernal Bridegroom says he will gash himself up, will make himself ugly, will howl in the streets: '[j]e veux devenir bien fou de rage (I want to become mad with rage)'.[3]

In 'Delirium I', Arthur Rimbaud's poetic voice apparently impersonates that of a 'Foolish Virgin' (taken to be Paul Verlaine) discussing her 'Infernal Bridegroom' (taken to be Rimbaud). However, before the reader accepts 'Delirium I' as a record of the

---

3 A. Rimbaud, *Complete Works*, 188, tr. A. Jary.

French poets' famous, gay love affair, it is worth recalling that poetic accounts of people's lives can be distortions, exagger-ations, or complete pretense. The reality of the life Verlaine and Rimbaud led may hardly appear in *A Season in Hell*, or in any of Rimbaud's poetry. Poets alter life in their poems as they wish – for artistic reasons, or for any number of motives. It is problematic working back from the poems to the poet's life: this is demonstrated by considering William Shakespeare's *Sonnets* and how they relate to the 'real' Shakespeare's relationship with the beloved youth and the 'Dark Lady', or when considering the 'real' Francesco Petrarch's relationship with the 'real' Laura de Sade, the subject of Petrarch's *Canzoniere*.

Remember, then, that in 'Delirium I: The Foolish Virgin' in *A Season in Hell*, a very clever and self-aware poet (Arthur Rimbaud) is impersonating a strange character called the 'Foolish Virgin' which may relate to Paul Verlaine. Also, if the reader swops the roles of the 'Foolish Virgin' and the 'Infernal Bride-groom', the poem is equally insightful. Even if this is biography or autobiography, it is a very peculiar kind of biography or auto-biography. Poems are seldom as straightforward as biographies (or novels) anyway; poems are distinct forms of expression with their own laws and needs. Rimbaud's poems, in particular, are highly idiosyncratic. Given the kind of poet that Rimbaud was, the kind of poems that he wrote, his personal aesthetics, his intense self-awareness (in life as in poetry), and his unique life-philosophy, one should not automatically see texts such as 'Delirium I' as biography.

Paul Verlaine also poeticized Arthur Rimbaud – most famously in poem 'À Arthur Rimbaud':

> Mortel, ange ET démon, autaunt dire Rimbaud,
> Tu mérites la prime place en ce mien livre,
> Bien que tel sot grimaud t'ait traité de ribaud
> Imberbe et de monstre en herbe et de potache ivre.

The poems of Paul Verlaine re-pay any visit, as the poems

selected for this book demonstrate. Verlaine is a poet who carved out his own niche in the history of poetry: his poems are instantly recognizable for their imagery and themes, and perhaps for their pure poetic approach, more than anything. Verlaine is a 'poet's poet'.

BIBLIOGRAPHY

BY PAUL VERLAINE

Forty Poems, tr. R. Gant & C. Apcher, Falcon Press, 1948
Œuvres poétiques complètes, ed. Y.-G. Le Dantec, Gallimard, 1951
The Sky Above the Roof, tr. B. Hill, Rupert Hart-Davis, 1957
Odeds en Son Honneur Élégies, Librairie Armand Colin, Paris, 1959
Selected Poems, tr. Joanna Richardson, Penguin, London, 1974
Fêtes galantes, ed. Jean Gaudon, Garnier-Flammarion, 1976
Femmes, Hombres, tr. A. Elliot, Anvil Press, London, 1979
One Hundred and One Poems, tr. N. Shapiro, University Press, Chicago, IL, 1999

ABOUT PAUL VERLANIE

E. Delahaye. *Rimbaud*, Messein, 1928
—. *Souveniers familiers à propos de Rimbaud, Verlaine et Germain Nouveau*, Messein, 1925
W. Fowlie. *Rimbaud*, University of Chicago Press, Chicago, 1965
—. *Rimbaud and Jim Morrison: The Rebel as Poet*, Souvenir, 1995
C.A. Hackett. *Rimbaud*, Hilary House, New York, NY, 1977
—. "Verlaine's Influence on Rimbaud", in Lloyd James Austin, ed. *Studies in Modern French Literature Presented to P. Mansell Jones*, Manchester University Press, Manchester, 1961, 163-180
J. & V. Hanson. *Verlaine, Prince of Poets*, Chatto & Windus, London, 1959
Mario Praz: *The Romantic Agony*, tr. A. Davidson, Oxford University Press, Oxford, 1933
Joanna Richardson. *Verlaine*, Weidenfeld & Nicolson, London, 1971
P. Schmidt. "Visions of Violence: Rimbaud and Verlaine", in G.

Stambolian, 228-242

George Stambolian & Elaine Marks, eds. *Homosexuality and French Literature: Cultural Contexts/ Critical Texts*, Cornell University Press, Ithaca, 1979

V.P. Underwood. *Verlaine et l'Angleterre*, Nizet, 1956

BY ARTHUR RIMBAUD

Œuvres, ed. Suzanne Bernard & André Guyaux, Garnier, 1981

Œuvres complètes, ed. Antoine Adam, Gallimard, 1972

Complete Works, Selected Letters, tr. Wallace Fowlie, University of Chicago Press, Chicago, 1966

Collected Poems, ed. Oliver Bernhard, Penguin, London, 1986

Illuminations, tr. Louise Varèse, New Directions, New York, NY, 1946

A Season In Hell, tr. Andrew Jary, Crescent Moon, 2007

Morning of Ecstasy: Selected Poems, tr. Andrew Jary, Crescent Moon, 2007

Arseny Tarkovsky

Life, Life

Selected Poems

Arseny Tarkovsky is the neglected Russian poet, father of the acclaimed film director Andrei Tarkovsky. This new book gathers together many of Tarkovsky's most lyrical and heartfelt poems, in Virginia Rounding's new, clear translations. Many of Tarkovsky's poems appeared in his son's films, such as *Mirror, Stalker, Nostalghia* and *The Sacrifice*. There is an introduction by Rounding, and a bibliography of both Arseny and Andrei Tarkovsky.

Illustrated. Bibliography and notes.
ISBN 9781861711144 Pbk   ISBN 9781861712660 Hbk

Beauties, Beasts, and Enchantment

CLASSIC FRENCH FAIRY TALES

Translated and with an Introduction
by Jack Zipes

A collection of 36 classic French fairy tales translated by renowned writer Jack Zipes. *Cinderella, Beauty and the Beast, Sleeping Beauty* and *Little Red Riding Hood* are among the classic fairy tales in this amazing book.
Includes illustrations from fairy tale collections.
Jack Zipes has written and published widely on fairy tales.

'Terrific... a succulent array of 17th and 18th century 'salon' fairy tales'
- *The New York Times Book Review*

'These tales are adventurous, thrilling in a way fairy tales are meant to be... The translation from the French is modern, happily free of archaic and hyperbolic language... a fine and sophisticated collection' - *New York Tribune*

'Enjoyable to read... a unique collection of French regional folklore' - *Library Journal*

'Charming stories accompanied by attractive pen-and-ink drawings' - *Chattanooga Times*

Introduction and illustrations 612pp. ISBN 9781861712510 Pbk ISBN 9781861713193 Hbk

CRESCENT MOON PUBLISHING

web: www.crmoon.com e-mail: cresmopub@yahoo.co.uk

ARTS, PAINTING, SCULPTURE

The Art of Andy Goldsworthy
Andy Goldsworthy: Touching Nature
Andy Goldsworthy in Close-Up
Andy Goldsworthy: Pocket Guide
Andy Goldsworthy In America
Land Art: A Complete Guide
The Art of Richard Long
Richard Long: Pocket Guide
Land Art In the UK
Land Art in Close-Up
Land Art In the U.S.A.
Land Art: Pocket Guide
Installation Art in Close-Up
Minimal Art and Artists In the 1960s and After
Colourfield Painting
Land Art DVD, TV documentary
Andy Goldsworthy DVD, TV documentary
The Erotic Object: Sexuality in Sculpture From Prehistory to the Present Day
Sex in Art: Pornography and Pleasure in Painting and Sculpture
Postwar Art
Sacred Gardens: The Garden in Myth, Religion and Art
Glorification: Religious Abstraction in Renaissance and 20th Century Art
Early Netherlandish Painting
Leonardo da Vinci
Piero della Francesca
Giovanni Bellini
Fra Angelico: Art and Religion in the Renaissance
Mark Rothko: The Art of Transcendence
Frank Stella: American Abstract Artist
Jasper Johns
Brice Marden
Alison Wilding: The Embrace of Sculpture
Vincent van Gogh: Visionary Landscapes
Eric Gill: Nuptials of God
Constantin Brancusi: Sculpting the Essence of Things
Max Beckmann
Caravaggio
Gustave Moreau
Egon Schiele: Sex and Death In Purple Stockings
Delizioso Fotografico Fervore: Works In Process 1
Sacro Cuore: Works In Process 2
The Light Eternal: J.M.W. Turner
The Madonna Glorified: Karen Arthurs

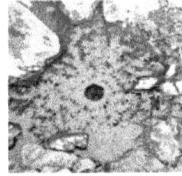

LITERATURE

J.R.R. Tolkien: The Books, The Films, The Whole Cultural Phenomenon
J.R.R. Tolkien: Pocket Guide
Tolkien's Heroic Quest
The *Earthsea* Books of Ursula Le Guin
Beauties, Beasts and Enchantment: Classic French Fairy Tales
German Popular Stories by the Brothers Grimm
Philip Pullman and *His Dark Materials*
Sexing Hardy: Thomas Hardy and Feminism
Thomas Hardy's *Tess of the d'Urbervilles*
Thomas Hardy's *Jude the Obscure*
Thomas Hardy: The Tragic Novels
Love and Tragedy: Thomas Hardy
The Poetry of Landscape in Hardy
Wessex Revisited: Thomas Hardy and John Cowper Powys
Wolfgang Iser: Essays and Interviews
Petrarch, Dante and the Troubadours
Maurice Sendak and the Art of Children's Book Illustration
Andrea Dworkin
Cixous, Irigaray, Kristeva: The *Jouissance* of French Feminism
Julia Kristeva: Art, Love, Melancholy, Philosophy, Semiotics and Psychoanalysis
Hélene Cixous I Love You: The *Jouissance* of Writing
Luce Irigaray: Lips, Kissing, and the Politics of Sexual Difference
Peter Redgrove: Here Comes the Flood
Peter Redgrove: Sex-Magic-Poetry-Cornwall
Lawrence Durrell: Between Love and Death, East and West
Love, Culture & Poetry: Lawrence Durrell
Cavafy: Anatomy of a Soul
German Romantic Poetry: Goethe, Novalis, Heine, Hölderlin
Feminism and Shakespeare
Shakespeare: Love, Poetry & Magic
The Passion of D.H. Lawrence
D.H. Lawrence: Symbolic Landscapes
D.H. Lawrence: Infinite Sensual Violence
Rimbaud: Arthur Rimbaud and the Magic of Poetry
The Ecstasies of John Cowper Powys
Sensualism and Mythology: The Wessex Novels of John Cowper Powys
Amorous Life: John Cowper Powys and the Manifestation of Affectivity (H.W. Fawkner)
Postmodern Powys: New Essays on John Cowper Powys (Joe Boulter)
Rethinking Powys: Critical Essays on John Cowper Powys
Paul Bowles & Bernardo Bertolucci
Rainer Maria Rilke
Joseph Conrad: *Heart of Darkness*
In the Dim Void: Samuel Beckett
Samuel Beckett Goes into the Silence
André Gide: Fiction and Fervour
Jackie Collins and the Blockbuster Novel
Blinded By Her Light: The Love-Poetry of Robert Graves
The Passion of Colours: Travels In Mediterranean Lands
Poetic Forms

POETRY

Ursula Le Guin: Walking In Cornwall
Peter Redgrove: Here Comes The Flood
Peter Redgrove: Sex-Magic-Poetry-Cornwall
Dante: Selections From the Vita Nuova
Petrarch, Dante and the Troubadours
William Shakespeare: Sonnets
William Shakespeare: Complete Poems
Blinded By Her Light: The Love-Poetry of Robert Graves
Emily Dickinson: Selected Poems
Emily Brontë: Poems
Thomas Hardy: Selected Poems
Percy Bysshe Shelley: Poems
John Keats: Selected Poems
Joh n Keats: Poems of 1820
D.H. Lawrence: Selected Poems
Edmund Spenser: Poems
Edmund Spenser: Amoretti
John Donne: Poems
Henry Vaughan: Poems
Sir Thomas Wyatt: Poems
Robert Herrick: Selected Poems
Rilke: Space, Essence and Angels in the Poetry of Rainer Maria Rilke
Rainer Maria Rilke: Selected Poems
Friedrich Hölderlin: Selected Poems
Arseny Tarkovsky: Selected Poems
Arthur Rimbaud: Selected Poems
Arthur Rimbaud: A Season in Hell
Arthur Rimbaud and the Magic of Poetry
Novalis: Hymns To the Night
German Romantic Poetry
Paul Verlaine: Selected Poems
Elizaethan Sonnet Cycles
D.J. Enright: By-Blows
Jeremy Reed: Brigitte's Blue Heart
Jeremy Reed: Claudia Schiffer's Red Shoes
Gorgeous Little Orpheus
Radiance: New Poems
Crescent Moon Book of Nature Poetry
Crescent Moon Book of Love Poetry
Crescent Moon Book of Mystical Poetry
Crescent Moon Book of Elizabethan Love Poetry
Crescent Moon Book of Metaphysical Poetry
Crescent Moon Book of Romantic Poetry
Pagan America: New American Poetry

MEDIA, CINEMA, FEMINISM and CULTURAL STUDIES

J.R.R. Tolkien: The Books, The Films, The Whole Cultural Phenomenon
J.R.R. Tolkien: Pocket Guide
The *Lord of the Rings* Movies: Pocket Guide
The Cinema of Hayao Miyazaki
Hayao Miyazaki: *Princess Mononoke*: Pocket Movie Guide
Hayao Miyazaki: *Spirited Away*: Pocket Movie Guide
Tim Burton : Hallowe'en For Hollywood
Ken Russell
Ken Russell: *Tommy*: Pocket Movie Guide
The Ghost Dance: The Origins of Religion
The Peyote Cult
Cixous, Irigaray, Kristeva: The *Jouissance* of French Feminism
Julia Kristeva: Art, Love, Melancholy, Philosophy, Semiotics and Psychoanalysis
Luce Irigaray: Lips, Kissing, and the Politics of Sexual Difference
Hélene Cixous I Love You: The *Jouissance* of Writing
Andrea Dworkin
'Cosmo Woman': The World of Women's Magazines
Women in Pop Music
HomeGround: The Kate Bush Anthology
Discovering the Goddess (Geoffrey Ashe)
The Poetry of Cinema
The Sacred Cinema of Andrei Tarkovsky
Andrei Tarkovsky: Pocket Guide
Andrei Tarkovsky: *Mirror*: Pocket Movie Guide
Andrei Tarkovsky: *The Sacrifice*: Pocket Movie Guide
Walerian Borowczyk: Cinema of Erotic Dreams
Jean-Luc Godard: The Passion of Cinema
Jean-Luc Godard: *Hail Mary*: Pocket Movie Guide
Jean-Luc Godard: *Contempt*: Pocket Movie Guide
Jean-Luc Godard: *Pierrot le Fou*: Pocket Movie Guide
John Hughes and Eighties Cinema
Ferris Bueller's Day Off: Pocket Movie Guide
Jean-Luc Godard: Pocket Guide
The Cinema of Richard Linklater
Liv Tyler: Star In Ascendance
Blade Runner and the Films of Philip K. Dick
Paul Bowles and Bernardo Bertolucci
Media Hell: Radio, TV and the Press
An Open Letter to the BBC
Detonation Britain: Nuclear War in the UK
Feminism and Shakespeare
Wild Zones: Pornography, Art and Feminism
Sex in Art: Pornography and Pleasure in Painting and Sculpture
Sexing Hardy: Thomas Hardy and Feminism

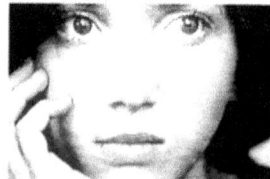

The Light Eternal is a model monograph, an exemplary job. The subject matter of the book is beautifully organised and dead on beam. (Lawrence Durrell)
It is amazing for me to see my work treated with such passion and respect. (Andrea Dworkin)

CRESCENT MOON PUBLISHING
P.O. Box 1312, Maidstone, Kent, ME14 5XU, Great Britain. www.crmoon.com

cresmopub@yahoo.co.uk   www.crescentmoon.org.uk

www.ingramcontent.com/pod-product-compliance
Lightning Source LLC
LaVergne TN
LVHW022341080426
835508LV00012BA/1300

* 9 7 8 1 8 6 1 7 1 9 5 6 0 *